RICK W

UNSHAKABLE

THRIVING NO MATTER WHAT HITS YOU

UNSHAKABLE: THRIVING NO MATTER WHAT HITS YOU
An Eight-Session Study for Small Groups or Individuals
Version 1.1

Published by Purpose Driven Publishers
23182 Arroyo Vista
Rancho Santa Margarita, CA 92688

ISBN: 978-1-4228-0436-0

Printed and bound in the United States of America.

TABLE OF CONTENTS

HOW TO USE THIS VIDEO CURRICULUM

Here is a brief explanation of the features of this study guide.

CHECKING IN:

You will open each meeting with an opportunity for everyone to check in with each other about how you are doing with the weekly assignments. Accountability is a key to success in this study!

KEY VERSE:

Each week you will find a key verse or Scripture passage for your group to read together. If someone in the group has a different translation, ask them to read it aloud so the group can get a bigger picture of the meaning of the passage.

VIDEO LESSON:

There is a video lesson for the group to watch together each week. Fill in the blanks in the lesson outlines as you watch the video, and be sure to refer back to these outlines during your discussion time.

DISCOVERY QUESTIONS:

Each video segment is complemented by several questions for group discussion. Please don't feel pressured to discuss every single question. There is no reason to rush through the answers. Give everyone ample opportunity to share their thoughts. If you don't get through all of the discussion questions, that's okay.

PUTTING IT INTO PRACTICE:

This is where the rubber meets the road. We don't want to be just hearers of the Word. We also need to be doers of the Word (James 1:22). These assignments are application exercises that will help you put into practice the truths you have discussed in the lesson.

PRAYER DIRECTION:

At the end of each session you will find suggestions for your group prayer time. Praying together is one of the greatest privileges of small group life. Please don't take it for granted.

A TIP FOR THE HOST:

The study guide material is meant to be your servant, not your master. The point is not to race through the sessions; the point is to take time to let God work in your lives. Nor is it necessary to "go around the circle" before you move on to the next question. Give people the freedom to speak, but don't insist on it. Your group will enjoy deeper, more open sharing and discussion if people don't feel pressured to speak up.

UNSHAKABLE

SESSION 1: WHEN YOU'RE PRESSURED TO CONFORM

We're beginning a study of how God tested Daniel through every stage of his life, from his teenage years all the way into retirement. And the practical lessons from Daniel's story will help every one of us to stand firm in our beliefs and develop a greater trust in God.

CHECKING IN:

If this is your first time meeting as a group, or if you have any new group members, be sure to introduce yourselves.

This week we're going to learn how to develop an unshakeable faith for those times when you feel pressured to conform.

KEY VERSE:

"If my people, who are called by my name, will humble themselves and pray and seek my face and turn from their wicked ways, then I will hear from heaven, and I will forgive their sin and will heal their land."

2 CHRONICLES 7:14 (NIV)

"Fire tests the purity of silver and gold, but the Lord tests the heart."

PROVERBS 17:3 (NLT)

BEFORE EVERY BLESSING, THERE'S A Testing.

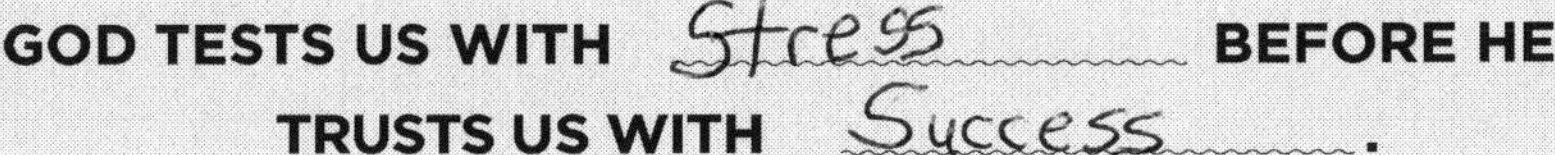

GOD TESTS US WITH Stress BEFORE HE TRUSTS US WITH Success.

"The king assigned them a daily amount of food and wine from the king's table. They were to be trained for three years, and after that they were to enter the king's service. But Daniel resolved not to defile himself with the royal food and wine, and he asked the chief official for permission not to defile himself this way."

DANIEL 1:5, 8 (NIV)

4 QUALITIES GOD LOOKS FOR IN YOUR LIFE

1.) Integrity **— Daniel never forgot who he was.**

"Do not conform yourselves to the standards of this world, but let God transform you inwardly by a complete change of your mind. Then you will be able to know the will of God."

ROMANS 12:2 (GNT)

2.) Discipline **— Daniel controlled his ego and his appetite.**

"But Daniel made up his mind not to eat the food and wine given to them by the king."

DANIEL 1:8 (TLB)

"Do not let any part of your body become an instrument of evil to serve sin. Instead, give yourselves completely to God, for you were dead, but now you have new life. So use your whole body as an instrument to do what is right for the glory of God."

ROMANS 6:13 (NLT)

3.) Courage — Daniel was willing to stand alone.

"Never follow a crowd in doing wrong, don't be swayed in your testimony by the mood of the majority."

EXODUS 23:2 (GW/TLB)

"Be on guard. Stand firm in the faith. Be courageous. Be strong."

1 CORINTHIANS 16:13 (NLT)

4.) Humility — Daniel was tactful with authority.

But Daniel resolved not to defile himself with the royal food and wine, and he asked the chief official for permission not to defile himself this way. Now God had caused the official to show favor and compassion to Daniel, but the official told Daniel, "I am afraid of my lord the king, who has assigned your food and drink. Why should he see you looking worse than the other young men your age? The king would then have my head because of you."

Daniel then said to the guard whom the chief official had appointed over Daniel, Hananiah, Mishael and Azariah, "Please test your servants for ten days: Give us nothing but vegetables to eat and water to drink. Then compare our appearance with that of the young men who eat the royal food, and treat your servants in accordance with what you see." So he agreed to this and tested them for ten days.

At the end of the ten days they looked healthier and better nourished than any of the young men who ate the royal food. So the guard took away their choice food and the wine they were to drink and gave them vegetables instead. At theend of the time set by the king to bring them into his service, the chief official presented them to Nebuchadnezzar. The king talked with them, and he found none equal to Daniel, Hananiah, Mishael and Azariah; so they entered the king's service.

DANIEL 1:8-16, 18-19 (NIV)

HOW TO MAKE A CASE TO AN AUTHORITY

1.) Develop a reputation for responsibility.

"Do you know a hard-working man?
He shall be successful and stand before kings!"
PROVERBS 22:29 (TLB)

2.) Be Humble, not Belligerent.

"When you stand before the king,
don't try to impress him and pretend to be important."
PROVERBS 25:6 (GNT)

3.) Don't be deceptive or manipulative.

"We reject all shameful deeds and underhanded methods.
We don't try to trick anyone or distort the word of God.
We tell the truth before God, and all who are honest know this."
2 CORINTHIANS 4:2 (NLT)

4.) Appeal to their goals and interests.

5.) Choose the right place, time, and words.

"A wise, mature person is known for his understanding.
The more pleasant his words, the more persuasive he is."
PROVERBS 16:21 (GNT)

6.) Trust God **if they reject your appeal.**

"And we know that in all things God works for the good of those who love him, who have been called according to his purpose."

ROMANS 8:28 (NIV)

Don't become partners with those who reject God. How can you make a partnership out of right and wrong? That'snot partnership; that'swar. Is light best friends with dark? Does Christ go strolling with the Devil? Do trust and mistrust hold hands? Who would think of setting up pagan idols in God's holy Temple? But that is exactly what we are, each of us a temple in whom God lives.Godhimself put it this way: "I'Illive in them, move into them; I'll be their God and they'll be my people. So leave the corruption and compromise . . . I'll be a Father to you; you'll be sons and daughters to me." . . . With promises like this to pull us on, dear friends, let'smake a clean break with everything that defiles or distracts us, both within and without. Let'smake our entire lives fit and holy temples for the worship of God.

2 CORINTHIANS 6:14–7:1 (THE MESSAGE)

DISCOVERY QUESTIONS:

1.) God's Word teaches us that before every blessing, there's a testing. How have you experienced this in your own life? What's an example of a time that God tested you with stress before he trusted you with success? How did going through that stressful situation affect the way you handled your success?

2.) Of the "4 Qualities That God Looks for in Your Life" (Integrity, discipline, courage, and humility), which one do you struggle with the most? What might help you get stronger in this area? How is your struggle related to your trust in God?

3.) Have you ever needed to make an appeal to an authority, asking for a decision to be changed? How did it go? How might you do it differently now that you have learned the way Daniel made an appeal?

PUTTING IT INTO PRACTICE:

Exodus 23:2 teaches us to *"Never follow a crowd in doing wrong"* (GW). What crowds in your life may tempt you to do the wrong thing? Why are you tempted to follow them?

How will this lesson help you to stand firm on God's truth? How can you apply what you've learned in this lesson to situations where you are tempted to follow the crowd?

PRAYER DIRECTION:

Do the following in your group prayer time and then on your own:

- Ask God to help you develop into a Daniel in your world, trusting in God no matter what your situation, no matter how much pressure you are under.
- Tell God you want him to develop each of these characteristics in you: integrity, humility, discipline, and courage. Take time to pray about each of these specifically and individually.
- Tell God you give him permission to do whatever it takes to help you become unafraid and unashamed, submitted to do whatever he asks you to do.

UNSHAKABLE

SESSION 2: WHEN YOUR BELIEFS ARE BELITTLED

CHECKING IN:

In Session 1, we talked about standing up to the people in your life who try to pressure you to compromise your faith. In what ways were you able to apply those lessons this week? Or what did you find the most helpful from last week's lesson?

This week we're going to learn how to develop an unshakeable faith for those times when your beliefs are belittled.

KEY VERSE:

"Wisdom brings strength, and knowledge gives power."

PROVERBS 24:5 (CEV)

Do yourself a favor and learn all you can;
then remember what you learn and you will prosper.
PROVERBS 19:8 (GNT)

Always remember what you have learned.
Your education is your life—guard it well.
PROVERBS 4:13 (GNT)

The king told Ashpenaz, the chief-of-staff, to bring some of the Israelites, the royal family, and the nobility. They were to be young men . . . well-informed, intelligent, and able to serve in the king's palace. They were to be taught the language and literature of the Babylonians . . .
They were to be trained for three years.
After that, they were to serve the king.
DANIEL 1:3-5 (GW)

Indoctrinate them in the Babylonian . . . lore
of magic and fortunetelling.
DANIEL 1:4 (THE MESSAGE)

God gave these four young men an unusual aptitude
for learning the literature and science of the time.
DANIEL 1:17 (NLT/TLB)

When the training period ordered by the king was completed, the chief of staff brought all the young men to King Nebuchadnezzar. The king talked with them, and no one impressed him as much as Daniel, Hananiah, Mishael, and Azariah. So they entered the royal service. Whenever the king consulted them in any matter requiring wisdom and balanced judgment, he found them ten times more capable than any of the magicians and enchanters in his entire kingdom.
DANIEL 1:18-20 (NLT)

HOW TO EXCEL IN MY EDUCATION
(and not lose my faith)

1.) **Decide in advance to** Stand for God

"Everyone who wants to live a godly life
in Christ Jesus will suffer persecution."

2 TIMOTHY 3:12 (NLT)

"Daniel made up his mind that he would not defile himself."

DANIEL 1:8 (NASB)

"Start with God—the first step in learning is bowing down to God; only fools thumb their noses at such wisdom and learning."

PROVERBS 1:7 (THE MESSAGE)

"Reverence for the Lord is an education in itself."

PROVERBS 15:33 (GNT)

2.) **Never stop** Learning .

ALL LEADERS ARE LEARNERS

"Wise men and women are always learning,
always listening for fresh insights."

PROVERBS 18:15 (THE MESSAGE)

"Study to shew thyself approved unto God,
a workman that needeth not to be ashamed."

2 TIMOTHY 2:15 (KJV)

"Those who get wisdom do themselves a favor,
and those who love learning will succeed."
PROVERBS 19:8 (NCV)

Book **KNOWLEDGE: INFORMATION GAINED FROM EDUCATION OR EXPERIENCE**

God **WISDOM: SEEING AND RESPONDING FROM GOD'S VIEWPOINT**

3.) Steep myself in God's Word **.**

"Study [God's Word] continually. Meditate on it day and night
so you will be sure to obey everything written in it.
Only then will you prosper and succeed in all you do."
JOSHUA 1:8 (NLT)

4.) Choose believers **as my best friends.**

"Do not be misled: 'Bad company corrupts good character.'"
1 CORINTHIANS 15:33 (NIV)

"Stay away from fools, or you won't learn a thing."

PROVERBS 14:7 (CEV)

"Fools show their stupidity by the way they live;
it's easy to see they have no sense."
ECCLESIASTES 10:3 (CEV)

"Happy are those who reject the advice of evil people, who do not follow the example of sinners or join those who have no use for God."
PSALM 1:1 (GNT)

5.) Stay Connected to a church, a small group, and a ministry.

"Let us not give up the habit of meeting together, as some are doing. Instead, let us encourage one another."

HEBREWS 10:25 (GNT)

6.) Remember that God will Reward me.

"'Blessed are you when people insult you, persecute you and falsely say all kinds of evil against you because of me. Rejoice and be glad, because great is your reward in heaven, for in the same way they persecuted the prophets who were before you.'"

MATTHEW 5:11-12 (NIV)

"Therefore God has highly exalted him and bestowed on him the name that is above every name, so that at the name of Jesus every knee should bow, in heaven and on earth and under the earth, and every tongue confess that Jesus Christ is Lord, to the glory of God the Father."

PHILIPPIANS 2:9-11 (ESV)

DISCOVERY QUESTIONS:

1.) Why is it so important to decide in advance that you will stand with God?

Be ready

2.) Biblical meditation is when we think about a Bible verse over and over again, asking God to give us insight. How has God spoken to you through specific Bible verses? Pick a verse from this week's lesson and mediate on it throughout the week.

3.) Why is it so important to stay connected with a church and a small group? How can other believers help you mature in your faith? How can you help others mature in their faith?

humility → ← to fear

4.) Talk about why this verse is true: *"Reverence for the Lord is an education in itself"* (Proverbs 15:33 GNT).

PUTTING IT INTO PRACTICE:

How will you steep yourself in God's Word this week? (Hint: See Discovery Question #2.)

Do you need to rethink any friendships? Is someone tempting you in the wrong direction? How can you develop strong Christian friendships?

God wants you to be a lifelong learner. What goals can you set for learning more? Perhaps it relates to Bible study or prayer, but it could be related to a skill or hobby.

PRAYER DIRECTION:

Do the following in your group prayer time and then on your own:

- Tell God you are committing in advance to stand for him. Ask God to support you and direct you as you take your stand, and ask him to help you maintain a loving and respectful attitude when you stand firm in your faith.
- Thank God that he has given you the capacity to learn and the freedom to explore. Ask him to help you to develop discernment, and to transform your knowledge into godly wisdom. Tell God you want to see things from his point of view.
- Tell God that you will steep yourself in his Word, and ask him to show you the benefits.
- Ask God to deepen your friendships with believers, including the people in your small group. And ask God to help you make new friends who will help you mature in faith, or whom you can help mature in faith.
- Thank God that you can be connected to a church, a small group, and a ministry. If you're disconnected in any of these areas, then ask God to guide you to the right connections.
- Thank God that he is for you, and wants you to succeed. Tell him that you come to him because you love him. Tell God that you trust in his promises and welcome any blessings he may give you.

UNSHAKABLE

SESSION 3: WHEN YOU'RE ASKED TO DO THE IMPOSSIBLE

CHECKING IN:

Last week we talked about how knowledge is information gained from education or experience, and wisdom is seeing and responding from God's point of view. When have you seen God transform your biblical knowledge into godly wisdom?

This week we're going to learn how to develop an unshakeable faith for those times when you're facing the impossible.

KEY VERSE:

"Nobody anywhere can do what you ask! . . .
What you're asking is impossible."

DANIEL 2:10-11 (THE MESSAGE)

One night during the second year of his reign, Nebuchadnezzar had such disturbing dreams that he couldn't sleep. He called in his magicians, enchanters, sorcerers, and astrologers, and he demanded that they tell him what he had dreamed. As they stood before the king, he said, "I have had a dream that deeply troubles me, and I must know what it means."

Then the astrologers answered the king in Aramaic, "Long live the king! Tell us the dream, and we will tell you what it means."

But the king said to the astrologers, "I am serious about this. If you don't tell me what my dream was and what it means, you will be torn limb from limb, and your houses will be turned into heaps of rubble! But if you tell me what I dreamed and what the dream means, I will give you many wonderful gifts and honors. Just tell me the dream and what it means!"

They said again, "Please, Your Majesty. Tell us the dream, and we will tell you what it means."

The king replied, "I know what you are doing! You're stalling for time because you know I am serious when I say, If you don't tell me the dream, you are doomed. So you have conspired to tell me lies, hoping I will change my mind. But tell me the dream, and then I'll know that you can tell me what it means."

The astrologers replied to the king, "No one on earth can tell the king his dream! And no king, however great and powerful, has ever asked such a thing of any magician, enchanter, or astrologer! The king's demand is impossible. No one except the gods can tell you your dream, and they do not live here among people."

The king was furious when he heard this, and he ordered that all the wise men of Babylon be executed. And because of the king's decree, men were sent to find and kill Daniel and his friends.

DANIEL 2:1-13 (NLT)

WHAT TO DO WHEN YOU'RE ASKED TO DO THE IMPOSSIBLE

1.) Don't panic **or** be afraid**.**

"When Arioch, the commander of the king's guard, came to kill them, Daniel handled the situation with wisdom and discretion."

DANIEL 2:14 (NLT)

2.) Ask why**.**

"[Daniel] asked Arioch, 'Why has the king issued such a harsh decree?'So Arioch told him all that had happened."

DANIEL 2:15 (NLT)

"Get the facts at any price."

PROVERBS 23:23 (TLB)

3.) Ask for time **to create a solution.**

"Daniel went at once to see the king and requested more time to tell the king what the dream meant."

DANIEL 2:16 (NLT)

4.) Enlist prayer support **from your friends.**

"Daniel returned home and told his three friends. Then he said, 'Pray that the God who rules from heaven will be merciful and explain this mystery, so that we and the others won't be put to death.'"

DANIEL 2:17-18 (CEV)

5.) Pray and expect God to give super natural help **.**

"If you need wisdom, ask our generous God, and he will give it to you. He will not rebuke you for asking. But when you ask him, be sure that you really expect him to tell you, for a doubtful mind will be as unsettled as a wave of the sea that is driven and tossed by the wind . . . If you don't ask with faith, don't expect the Lord to give you any solid answer."

JAMES 1:5-8 (NLT/TLB)

6.) Worship God **!**

"During the night the mystery was revealed to Daniel in a vision. Then Daniel praised the God of heaven."

DANIEL 2:19 (NIV)

7.) Use what God showed you to Save others **.**

"So Daniel went to Arioch, whom the king had commanded to execute the royal advisers. He said to him, 'Don't put them to death. Take me to the king, and I will tell him what his dream means.'"

DANIEL 2:24 (GNT)

"Arioch quickly took Daniel to the king and said, 'I have found one of the captives from Judah who will tell the king the meaning of his dream!' The king said to Daniel (also known as Belteshazzar), 'Is this true? Can you tell me what my dream was and what it means?'"

DANIEL 2:25-26 (NLT)

8.) point people to God.

"Daniel replied, 'No wise man, enchanter, magician or diviner can explain to the king the mystery he has asked about, but there is a God in heaven who reveals mysteries . . . As for me, this mystery has been revealed to me, not because I have greater wisdom than anyone else alive, but so that Your Majesty may know the interpretation and that you may understand what went through your mind.'"

DANIEL 2:27-30 (NIV)

"Then King Nebuchadnezzar bowed to the ground and gave orders for sacrifices and offerings to be made to Daniel. The king said, "Your God is the greatest of all gods, the Lord over kings, and the one who reveals mysteries. I know this because you have been able to explain this mystery."

DANIEL 2:46-47 (GNT)

"Then the king appointed Daniel to a high position and gave him many valuable gifts.HemadeDaniel ruler over the whole province of Babylon."

DANIEL 2:48 (NLT)

DISCOVERY QUESTIONS:

1.) Share an example of a time you had to face something impossible. How did God help you overcome it? How do you think the eight steps taught in this lesson will help you with the next impossible situation you face?

2.) Talk about why it's important to ask "Why?" and get the facts first when you are asked to do the impossible. Why would God want you to ask for more time to create a solution?

3.) What are the benefits of worshipping God when you face an impossible task? Why would he want you to do that?

PUTTING IT INTO PRACTICE:

If you are facing an impossible situation right now, create a plan for confronting it based on the steps above. If you are not in an impossible situation right now, think about a situation from your past and discuss how you might handle it differently now.

Start praying this week about your impossible situation, with the expectation that God will give you his supernatural help. If you are not facing something impossible right now, help someone else pray through his or her situation.

How can you use the lessons from one of your impossible situations to point someone else to God?

PRAYER DIRECTION:

Do the following in your group prayer time and then on your own:

- Tell God that you will walk in faith during impossible situations, trusting that he is with you and working through your circumstances. In faith, commit to taking your fear, worry, and any feelings of panic directly to God.
- Commit to God that you will always respectfully ask "why" in order to determine what the end goal is. Ask God to help you get the time you need to come up with a solution. And tell God you will patiently wait to hear from him about the solution. Tell God you will faithfully expect him to give you supernatural help.
- Worship God through your prayers. Tell him how much you love and appreciate him, and that you know he has your best interest at heart.
- Ask God to put you in situations where you can share what you have learned with others and point them to God.
- Ask God to remind you of this prayer whenever you start to panic or worry about an impossible situation.

SESSION 4: WHEN THE HEAT IS ON

CHECKING IN:

In Session 3, we talked about following the biblical steps for walking through an impossible situation. What did God show you this week as you expected him to give you his supernatural help?

This week we're going to learn how to develop an unshakeable faith for those times when the heat is on.

KEY VERSE:

"If we are thrown into the blazing furnace, the God whom we serve is able to save us."

DANIEL 3:17 (NLT)

King Nebuchadnezzar made a gold statue ninety feet tall and nine feet wide and set it up on the plain of Dura in the province of Babylon. Then he sent messages to the high officers, officials, governors, advisers, treasurers, judges, magistrates, and all the provincial officials to come to the dedication of the statue he had set up. So all these officials came and stood before the statue King Nebuchadnezzar had set up.

Then a herald shouted out, "People of all races and nations and languages, listen to the king's command! When you hear the sound of the horn, flute, zither, lyre, harp, pipes, and other musical instruments, bow to the ground to worship King Nebuchadnezzar's gold statue. Anyone who refuses to obey will immediately be thrown into a blazing furnace."

So at the sound of the musical instruments, all the people, whatever their race or nation or language, bowed to the ground and worshiped the gold statue that King Nebuchadnezzar had set up.

DANIEL 3:1-7 (NLT)

But some officials went to the king and accused some of the Jews of refusing to worship!

"Your Majesty," they said to him, "you made a law that everyone must fall down and worship the gold statue when the band begins to play, and that anyone who refuses will be thrown into a flaming furnace. But there are some Jews out there—Shadrach, Meshach, and Abednego, whom you have put in charge of Babylonian affairs—who have defied you, refusing to serve your gods or to worship the gold statue you set up."

Then Nebuchadnezzar, in a terrible rage, ordered Shadrach, Meshach, and Abednego to be brought in before him.

"Is it true, O Shadrach, Meshach, and Abednego," he demanded, "that you are refusing to serve my gods or to worship the gold statue I set up? I'll give you one more chance. When the music plays, if you fall down and worship the statue, all will be well. But if you refuse, you will be thrown into a flaming furnace within the hour. And what god can deliver you out of my hands then?"

DANIEL 3:8-15 (TLB)

WHAT SHOULD I DO WHEN THE HEAT IS ON?

1.) Don't worry about Defending myself.

"Shadrach, Meshach, and Abednego answered and said to the king, 'O Nebuchadnezzar, we have no need to answer you in this matter.'"

DANIEL 3:16 (ESV)

2.) Remember that God has the power to Save me.

"If we are thrown into the blazing furnace, the God whom we serve is able to save us."

DANIEL 3:17 (NLT)

3.) Believe that God will save me.

"He will save us from your power, O king."

DANIEL 3:17 (NCV)

4.) I announce my Loyalty to God no matter what.

"But even if God does not save us, we want you, O king, to know this: We will not serve your gods or worship the gold statue you have set up."

DANIEL 3:18 (NCV)

Nebuchadnezzar was so furious with Shadrach, Meshach, and Abednego that his face became distorted with rage. He commanded that the furnace be heated seven times hotter than usual. Then he ordered some of the strongest men of the army to bind Shadrach, Meshach, and Abednego and throw them into the blazing furnace. So they tied them up and threw them into the furnace, fully dressed in their pants, turbans, robes, and other garments. And because the king, in his anger, had demanded such a hot fire in the furnace, the flames killed the soldiers as they threw the three men in. So Shadrach, Meshach, and Abednego, securely tied, fell into the roaring flames.

DANIEL 3:19-23 (NLT)

WHAT HAPPENS WHEN I TRUST GOD IN THE FURNACE?

1.) God will walk through fire **with me.**

"Then King Nebuchadnezzar leaped to his feet in amazement and asked his advisers, 'Weren't there three men that we tied up and threw into the fire?' They replied, 'Certainly, Your Majesty.' He said, 'Look! I see four men walking around in the fire, unbound and unharmed, and the fourth looks like a son of the gods.'"

DANIEL 3:24-25 (NIV)

[Jesus said:] "I am with you always, to the very end of the age."

MATTHEW 28:20 (NIV)

2.) **God will** Burn off **everything tying me down.**

"I have refined you, but not as silver is refined.
Rather, I have refined you in the furnace of suffering."
ISAIAH 48:10 (NLT)

3.) **God will give me a new** Freedom**.**

"You let captors set foot on our neck;
we went through fire and water;
then you led us out to freedom."
PSALM 66:12 (NABRE)

4.) **God will make sure I come out** unharmed**.**

Then Nebuchadnezzar came as close as he could to the door of the flaming furnace and shouted: "Shadrach, Meshach, and Abednego, servants of the Most High God, come out! Come here!" So Shadrach, Meshach, and Abednego stepped out of the fire. Then the high officers, officials, governors, and advisers crowded around them and saw that the fire had not touched them. Not a hair on their heads was singed, and their clothing was not scorched. They didn't even smell of smoke!
DANIEL 3:26-27 (NLT)

5.) It will bring unbelivers **to God.**

"Then Nebuchadnezzar said, 'Praise be to the God of Shadrach, Meshach and Abednego, who has sent his angel and rescued his servants! They trusted in him and defied the king's command and were willing to give up their lives rather than serve or worship any god except their own God.'"

DANIEL 3:28 (NIV)

"'So I now give this command: Anyone from any nation or language who says anything against the God of Shadrach, Meshach, and Abednego will be torn apart and have his house turned into a pile of stones. No other god can save his people like this.' Then the king promoted Shadrach, Meshach, and Abednego in the area of Babylon."

DANIEL 3:29-30 (NCV)

6.) God will reward my faith **in Heaven.**

"We must each be careful how we build, because Christ is the only foundation. Whatever we build on that foundation will be tested by fire . . . We will be rewarded if our building is left standing. But if it is destroyed by the fire, we will lose everything. Yet we ourselves will be saved, like someone escaping from flames."

1 CORINTHIANS 3:10-15 (CEV)

DISCOVERY QUESTIONS:

1.) When we are criticized for what we believe, often our first reaction is defensiveness. But Daniel teaches us to trust God to defend us. What would that look like? Would you rather defend yourself or be defended by the God of the universe? Why? How can you develop trust that God will defend you?

2.) Isaiah 43:2 says, *"When you go through deep waters and great trouble, I will be with you . . . When you walk through the fire of oppression you will not be burned up"* (TLB).

Talk about a difficult time when you felt God's presence and you knew, without a doubt, that he was right there with you in the fire.

3.) What are some things God has "burned off" from your life? Why do you think he did that? How have you been different since then? How have your priorities changed?

PUTTING IT INTO PRACTICE:

Jesus will always be with me, even in the fire.

"I am with you always, to the very end of the age."

MATTHEW 28:20 (NIV)

God is refining me in the fire to help me mature.

"I have refined you but not as silver is refined.
Rather, I have refined you in the furnace of suffering."

ISAIAH 48:10 (NLT)

God is leading me through the fire to freedom.

"We went through fire and water;
then you led us out to freedom."

PSALM 66:12 (NABRE)

God is protecting me in the fire.

"Not a hair on their heads was singed, and their clothing was not scorched. They didn't even smell of smoke!"

DANIEL 3:27 (NLT)

God can be trusted when I'm in the fire.

"Then Nebuchadnezzar said, 'Praise be to the God of Shadrach, Meshach and Abednego, who has sent his angel and rescued his servants. They trusted in him.'"

DANIEL 3:28 (NIV)

Jesus will be my only foundation once I'm through the fire.

"Christ is the only solid foundation. Whatever we build on that foundation will be tested by fire . . . We will be rewarded if our building is left standing."

1 CORINTHIANS 3:11-12, 14 (CEV)

PRAYER DIRECTION:

As you pray silently, thank God for his promise to stay with you throughout the fires of life. Ask God to show you anything that's holding you back and needs to be "burned off" in the flames. Finally, ask God to continue to refine you in the midst of trials —whether it's a current trial or one to come in the future—and ask for strength to continually trust him in the midst of whatever difficult time may come.

Do the following in your group prayer time and then on your own:

- Tell God you will trust him to defend you and that you will believe he is doing that.
- Praise God, telling him that you know he has the power to save you and that you believe he will save you. Ask him to help you mature in this belief.
- Tell God you will remain loyal to him no matter what. "God, no matter what I face, I will never serve false gods, only you—the one, true God."

UNSHAKABLE

SESSION 5: WHEN GOD TESTS YOU WITH SUCCESS

CHECKING IN:

Last week we talked about trusting God when the heat is on. Consider how you are doing with the idea that, *"If we are thrown into the blazing furnace, the God whom we serve is able to save us"* (Daniel 3:17 NLT).

This week we're going to learn how to develop an unshakeable faith for the times you are tested by success.

KEY VERSE:

"A hot furnace tests silver and gold,

and people are tested by the praise they receive."

PROVERBS 27:21 (NCV)

WHAT GETS US INTO TROUBLE

1.) We get Comfortable and complacent with success.

"I, Nebuchadnezzar, was living in peace and prosperity. I was taking it easy…, without a care in the world"
DANIEL 4:4 (TLB/THE MESSAGE)

"I was saying to myself, 'Just look at this wonderful capital city [Babylon] that I have built by my own power and for my own glory!'"
DANIEL 4:30 (CEV)

"Everyone with a proud heart is detestable to the Lord; be assured, he will not go unpunished."
PROVERBS 16:5 (CSB)

2.) We don't pay attention to the Warning Signs.

"Therefore, Your Majesty, be pleased to accept my advice: Renounce your sins by doing what is right, and your wickedness by being kind to the oppressed. It may be that then your prosperity will continue."
DANIEL 4:27 (NIV)

TO MAINTAIN SUCCESS, I NEED TO:

- repent - change your way of thinking
- Serve the poor

*"If you want to be happy, be kind to the poor;
it is a sin to despise anyone."*
PROVERBS 14:21 (GNT)

*"Whoever mistreats the poor insults their Maker,
but whoever is kind to the needy honors God."*
PROVERBS 14:31 (NCV)

*"Those who shut their ears to the cries of the poor
will be ignored in their own time of need."*
PROVERBS 21:13 (NLT)

3.) We put off doing what we know is right.

All this happened to King Nebuchadnezzar. Just twelve months later, he was walking on the balcony of the royal palace in Babylon and boasted . . . The words were no sooner out of his mouth than a voice out of heaven spoke, "This is the verdict on you, King Nebuchadnezzar: Your kingdom is taken from you. You will be driven out of human company and live with the wild animals. You will eat grasslike an ox. The sentence is for seven seasons, enough time to learn that the High God rules human kingdoms and puts whomever he wishes in charge." It happened at once.
DANIEL 4:28-33 (THE MESSAGE)

STEPS TO RECOVERY

1.) Look up to God.

"After this time had passed, I, Nebuchadnezzar, looked up to heaven. My sanity returned."

DANIEL 4:34 (NLT)

2.) Wake up to God's greatness and Start worshipping

"My sanity returned, and I praised and worshiped the Most High and honored the one who lives forever."

DANIEL 4:34 (NLT)

We get better when we replace pride with praise.

TRUTHS ABOUT GOD THAT STABILIZE MY LIFE

-God's Kingdom will outlast everything I do.

"[God's] *rule is everlasting, and his kingdom is eternal!"*

DANIEL 4:34 (NLT)

-God's approval matters more than all the others.

"All the people of the earth are nothing compared to him."

DANIEL 4:35 (NLT)

-God's power is absolute.

"He does as he pleases among the angels of heaven and among the people of the earth. No one can stop him . . . And those who walk in pride he is able to humble."

DANIEL 4:35, 37 (NLT/NIV)

"At that time my mind was healed, and once again I became the ruler of my glorious kingdom. My advisors and officials returned to me, and I had greater power than ever before. That's why I say: 'Praise and honor the King who rules from heaven! Everything he does is honest and fair.'"

DANIEL4:36-37 (CEV)

-God never makes any mistakes.

3.) Tell others how God has saved and changed you.

"King Nebuchadnezzar sent this message to the people of every race and nation and language throughout the world: 'Peace and prosperity to you! I want you all to know about the miraculous signs and wonders the Most High God has performed for me.'"

DANIEL 4:1-2 (NLT)

DISCOVERY QUESTIONS:

1.) What happens when we replace pride with praise? Why do we have trouble doing that sometimes?

Because we are human

2.) Talk about how each of these truths can translate into your life—and why believing them will stabilize your life.

- **God's Kingdom will outlast everything I do.**

- **God's approval matters more than all the others.**

- **God's power is absolute.**

PUTTING IT INTO PRACTICE:

Ask yourself some serious questions:

Why is it sometimes harder to handle success than failure? Why is success a test?

Have you become comfortable and complacent with success? If so, how can you re-energize your faith and your life?

Have you been ignoring any warning signs? If there are any, what will you do now that you've acknowledged them?

What do you know God wants you to do but you haven't done yet? What will it take for you to do what God has told you to do (if this applies)?

PRAYER DIRECTION:

One person can lead this prayer for your group, or participants can pray this to themselves silently:

> *God, I'm sorry for the times I've acted like I knew what was best. I want to wake up to your greatness, and I want to start worshiping you. I want to focus on you. I want to replace my pride with praise. Help me to seek your approval alone. And help me to tell others how you have changed and saved me. In your name I pray, Amen.*

UNSHAKABLE

SESSION 6: ARE YOU LEARNING FROM THOSE WHO CAME BEFORE YOU?

CHECKING IN:

Last week we talked about how success is a test that can shake our faith. What are some ways you've started replacing pride with praise?

This week we'll see how we can develop an unshakeable faith by learning from people who came before us and from people who are just ahead of us in spiritual growth.

KEY VERSE:

"Always remember what you have learned. Your education is your life—guard it well."

PROVERBS 4:13 (GNT)

King Belshazzar gave a great banquet for a thousand of his nobles and drank wine with them. While Belshazzar was drinking his wine, he gave orders to bring in the gold and silver goblets that Nebuchadnezzar his father had taken from the temple in Jerusalem, so that the king and his nobles, his wives and his concubines might drink from them. So they brought in the gold goblets that had been taken from the temple of God in Jerusalem, and the king and his nobles, his wives and his concubines drank from them. As they drank the wine, they praised the gods of gold and silver, of bronze, iron, wood and stone.

"Suddenly the fingers of a human hand appeared and wrote on the plaster walls of the wall, near the lampstand in the royal palace. The king watched the hand as it wrote. His face turned pale and he was so frightened that his legs became weak and his knees were knocking.

DANIEL 5:1-6 (NIV)

This is the message that was written:
Mene, Mene, Tekel, and Parsin.

DANIEL 5:25 (NLT)

Then Belshazzar ordered that Daniel be dressed in purple and wear a gold chain on his neck. He made Daniel the thirdhighest ruler in the kingdom. That night King Belshazzar of Babylon was killed. Darius the Mede took over the kingdom. He was 62 years old.

DANIEL 5:29-31 (GW)

Always remember what you have learned.
Your education is your life—guard it well.

PROVERBS 4:13 (GNT)

HOW CAN I BECOME WISE LIKE DANIEL?

1.) Make a commitment to never stop Learning.

"Commit yourself to instruction;
listen carefully to words of knowledge."

PROVERBS 23:12 (NLT)

"f an ax is dull and its edge is unsharpened,
more strength is needed, but skill will bring success."

ECCLESIASTES 10:10 (NIV)

"Do yourself a favor and learn all you can;
then remember what you learn and you will prosper."

PROVERBS 19:8 (GNT)

2.) Learn the lessons of the prior generations.

"Ask the former generation and find out what their ancestors learned,
for we were born only yesterday and know nothing."

JOB 8:8-9 (NIV)

The 4 Relationships You Need to Become Wise

- mentors
- role models
- partners
- friends

3.) **Maintain a** humble Attitude **that honors God.**

"Reverence for the Lord is an education in itself.
You must be humble before you can ever receive honors."
PROVERBS 15:33 (GNT)

"God opposes the proud but gives grace to the humble."
JAMES 4:6 (NLT)

4.) **Refuse to fill my mind with** Garbage **.**

5.) **Put into practice** what Ive already learned**.**

I haven't learned it **until I** do it **.**

"You are his successor, O Belshazzar, and you knew all this,
yet you have not humbled yourself.
For you have proudly defied the Lord of heaven."
DANIEL 5:22-23 (NLT)

IF I DON'T Humbly learn **FROM THE GENERATIONS BEFORE ME, I WILL END UP MAKING THE** Exact same mistakes **.**

"Some of these people have missed
the most important thing in life—they don't know God."
1 TIMOTHY 6:21 (TLB)

DISCOVERY QUESTIONS:

1.) What are some things you've learned from previous generations?

2.) Who is the wisest person you've ever known? What made that person wise? How have you benefitted from that person's wisdom?

3.) Discuss what this verse teaches about becoming wise:

"Some people have missed the most important thing in life—they don't know God"

1 TIMOTHY 6:21 (TLB)

4.) What does it mean to maintain a humble attitude toward God?

PUTTING IT INTO PRACTICE:

Spend a few minutes and think through some basic steps that you can take now that will help you to become (or improve at being) a lifelong learner.

Pastor Rick taught that we could learn from different types of relationships: mentors, role models, partners, and friends. Put one name next to each one of these relationships—someone who will help you learn and grow spiritually.

Mentor: ______________________________

Role Model: ______________________________

Partner: ______________________________

Friend: ______________________________

In the case of partners and friends, you already have existing relationships, but talk to them about how or what you want to learn from them. In the case of a mentor, think about how you can approach and ask that person to fulfill this role. The mentorship doesn't have to be time-consuming; you could just meet occasionally. In the case of a role model, list the qualities that you want to learn from that person, and then take note of how this person exhibits those qualities. And a role model could even be a person you meet through a Christian biography, helping you learn from past generations.

PRAYER DIRECTION:

Do the following in your group prayer time and then on your own:

- Tell God you want to humbly learn from others. Ask him to guide you toward the people you should learn from and what he wants you to learn.
- Ask God to bring to mind people who could help you learn—a mentor, role model, partner, or friend.
- Ask God if you should offer to mentor or teach a specific person.
- Ask God for wisdom and discernment as you learn, so that you are taking in what is beneficial and not absorbing "garbage" that will distract you from your purpose.
- Tell God that you are committed to putting what you learn into practice because you know that just having knowledge will not make a difference in your life if you don't apply it. Ask God to guide you so that you don't make the same mistakes over again.
- Tell God that you want to mature your faith to become unshakeable by learning from others and by learning how to apply his wisdom to your life.

UNSHAKABLE

SESSION 7: WILL YOU STAND STRONG FOR GOD PUBLICLY?

CHECKING IN:

Last week we talked about committing to a lifetime of learning. How have you decided to apply that in your life? What goals have you set for yourself?

This week we're going to see how we can develop an unshakeable faith that empowers us to stand up for God, even against opposition.

KEY VERSE:

"Never be ashamed to tell others about our Lord . . .
With the strength God gives you, be ready to suffer
with me for the sake of the Good News."

2 TIMOTHY 1:8 (NLT)

[King Belshazzar] made Daniel the third-highest ruler in the kingdom. That night King Belshazzar of Babylon was killed. Darius the Mede took over the kingdom. He was 62 years old.

DANIEL 5:29-30 (GW)

So the administrators and high officers went to the king and said, "Long live King Darius! We are all in agreement—we administrators, officials, high officers, advisers, and governors—that the king should make a law that will be strictly enforced. Give orders that for the next thirty days any person who prays to anyone, divine or human—except to you, Your Majesty—will be thrown into the den of lions. And now, Your Majesty, issue and sign this law so it cannot be changed, an official law of the Medes and Persians that cannot be revoked." So King Darius signed the law.

DANIEL 6:6-9 (NLT)

When Daniel learned that the law had been signed, he went home and knelt down as usual in his upstairs room, with its windows wide open toward Jerusalem. He prayed three times a day, just as he had always done, giving thanks to his God. Then the officials went together to Daniel's house and found him praying and asking for God's help.

DANIEL 6:10-11 (NLT)

WHY WAS DANIEL UNAFRAID TO STAND OUT AND SPEAK UP FOR GOD PUBLICLY?

1.) He remembered that God was Faithful **in past tests.**

2.) He had a Conversation with God **three times a day.**

The key to standing strong is kneeling often.

3.) He knew the rewards **were greater than the** risk**.**

6 WAYS I BENEFIT EVERY TIME I STAND FOR GOD

1.) It's a victory Over fear**.**

F - False

E - Evidence

A - Appearing

R - Real

"Lord, listen to their threats. Lord, help us, your servants, to speak your word without fear."

ACTS 4:29 (NCV)

2.) **It builds my** faith **and** Character **.**

COURAGE IS NOT THE ABSENCE OF FEAR

COURAGE IS DOING THE RIGHT THING IN SPITE OF YOUR FEAR

"Never be ashamed to tell others about our Lord . . . With the strength God gives you, be ready to suffer with me for the sake of the Good News."

2 TIMOTHY 1:8 (NLT)

3.) **It gives God a chance to** do a miracle **.**

At the first light of dawn, the king got up and hurried to the lions' den. When he came near the den, he called to Daniel in an anguished voice, "Daniel, servant of the living God, has your God, whom you serve continually, been able to rescue you from the lions?" Daniel answered, "May the king live forever! My God sent his angel, and he shut the mouths of the lions. They have not hurt me, because I was found innocent in his sight. Nor have I ever done any wrong before you, Your Majesty!" The king was overjoyed and gave orders to lift Daniel out of the den. And when Daniel was lifted from the den, no wound was found on him, because he had trusted in his God."

DANIEL 6:19-23 (NIV)

4.) **It encourages** other believers **to stand up.**

"Because of my imprisonment, most of the believers here have gained confidence . . . and they have become more and more bold in telling others about Christ."

PHILIPPIANS 1:14 (NLT/TLB)

5.) It's a powerful example to unbelievers**.**

"Then King Darius wrote to the people of all nations, races, and languages on earth: 'Greetings! I command that throughout my empire everyone should fear and respect Daniel's God. He is a living God, and he will rule forever. His kingdom will never be destroyed, and his power will never come to an end. He saves and rescues; he performs wonders and miracles in heaven and on earth. He saved Daniel from being killed by the lions." Daniel prospered during the reign of Darius and the reign of Cyrus the Persian.'"

DANIEL 6:25-28 (GNT)

6.) I will be rewarded in eternity**.**

"Count yourselves blessed every time people put you down or throw you out or speak lies about you to discredit me. What it means is that the truth is too close for comfort and they are uncomfortable. You can be glad when that happens—give a cheer, even!—for though they don't like it, I do! And all heaven applauds. And know that you are in good company. My prophets and witnesses have always gotten into this kind of trouble."

MATTHEW 5:11-12 (THE MESSAGE)

DISCOVERY QUESTIONS:

1.) Pastor Rick taught that Fear = False Evidence Appearing Real. Talk about a time when you found that to be true. Looking back, how would you face that fear now? What does that insight teach you about how to face fear in the future?

2.) Talk about a time that prayer helped you boldly and confidently handle something you were fearful about.

3.) Standing up for God can be a powerful example for believers and unbelievers alike. When have you seen a fellow believer stand up for what he or she believed? What was the result of that person's courage? How did that public stand for God impact you?

4.) Daniel's strength and courage came from his daily conversations with God. How does having a daily, intentional prayer time help you grow closer to God? When and why do you find it so difficult to pray, even though you know it is important?

PUTTING IT INTO PRACTICE:

Make a commitment to spend at least five minutes in intentional prayer each day this week. If you already do this, tell the rest of the group how that has helped you and how you have stayed consistent—or how you've handled the times of inconsistency.

Help each other be accountable by planning to come to the Bible study next week with a report on how things went. Make a specific plan for contacting each other during the week, encouraging others in the group to pray each day.

As you regularly spend time praying to God, talking with fellow believers, reading and studying the Bible, and becoming bolder in your faith, you'll be prepared to stand up for your beliefs publicly. The stronger your friendship with Jesus, the more natural it will be.

PRAYER DIRECTION:

Do the following in your group prayer time and then on your own:

- Tell God that you want to have a more consistent relationship with him and tell him you want to make prayer an intentional, consistent part of your daily lifestyle.
- Tell God that no matter what it takes, you want his help in building a practice of consistent daily prayer until it becomes a habit. If you already are consistently praying daily, ask God to deepen your prayer life, and ask him to show you someone that you can help grow in this area.
- Ask God to help you develop an unshakeable faith for future circumstances when you will need to stand up for what you believe.
- Ask God to guide you to other believers who will stand alongside you and encourage you as you take a stand—and to believers who need your encouragement to take a stand, too.

UNSHAKABLE

SESSION 8: THE KIND OF PRAYER GOD ANSWERS

CHECKING IN:

Last week we talked about the importance of daily conversation with God, and how our consistent conversations with God help us to stand boldly for God. How did things go this week? How was your prayer life this week? How did prayer help you approach each day?

This week we're going to talk about the kind of prayer that God answers. As we trust God to answer our prayers, our faith will mature and become unshakeable.

KEY VERSE:

"If my people, who are called by my name, will humble themselves and pray and seek my face and turn from their wicked ways, then I will hear from heaven, and I will forgive their sin and will heal their land."

2 CHRONICLES 7:14 (NIV)

HOW TO PRAY IN A CRISIS

1.) Let God speak to me before I speak to him **.**

"It was the first year of the reign of Darius the Mede, the son of Ahasuerus, who became king of the Babylonians. During the first year of his reign, I, Daniel, learned from reading the word of the Lord, as revealed to Jeremiah the prophet, that Jerusalem must lie desolate for seventy years."

DANIEL 9:1-2 (NLT)

"For this is what the Lord says: 'When Babylon's seventy years are completed, I'll take note of you and will fulfill my good promises to you by bringing you back to this place. For I know the plans that I have for you,' declares the Lord, 'plans for well-being, and not for calamity, in order to give you a future and a hope. When you call out to me and come and pray to me, I'll hear you.'"

JEREMIAH 29:10-12 (ISV)

2 Factors to Fulfilling My Purpose in Life:

- God's timing
- My Praying

"You do not have what you want because you do not ask God for it."

JAMES 4:2 (GNT)

2.) **Focus** my attention **on God.**

"Then I turned my face to the Lord God, seeking him."

DANIEL 9:3 (ESV)

"I love those who love me, and those who seek me find me."

PROVERBS 8:17 (NIV)

"You will . . . find me when you seek me with all your heart."

JEREMIAH 29:13 (NIV)

"[God] rewards those who earnestly seek him."

HEBREWS 11:6 (NIV)

"Seek the Kingdom of God above all else,
and he will give you everything you need."

LUKE 12:31 (NLT)

3.) **Express my desires with** emotion**.**

"[I] looked to [God] for help. I prayed, pleaded."

DANIEL 9:3 (GW)

"I poured out my heart, baring my soul to God, my God."

DANIEL 9:3 (THE MESSAGE)

"The people of Israel and Judah will come together.
They will cry and look for the Lord their God.
Those people will ask how to go to Jerusalem
and will start in that direction."

JEREMIAH 50:4-5 (NCV)

4.) **Demonstrate my** Seriousness**.**

"As I prayed, I fasted and wore rough sackcloth,
and I sprinkled myself with ashes."

DANIEL 9:3 (TLB)

5.) **Thank God for his** Love and promises**.**

"I prayed . . . 'O Lord, you are a great and awesome God!
You always fulfill your covenant and keep your promises
of unfailing love to those who love you and obey your commands.'"

DANIEL 9:4 (NLT)

"Lord God, you are merciful and forgiving,
even though we have rebelled against you."

DANIEL 9:9 (CEV)

6.) Humbly confess **my sin.**

"We have sinned and done wrong. We have rebelled against you and scorned your commands and regulations. We have refused to listen to your servants the prophets, who spoke on your authority to our kings and princes and ancestors and to all the people of the land."

DANIEL 9:5-6 (NLT)

"We are covered with shame . . . because of our unfaithfulness to you. We and our kings, our princes and our ancestors are covered with shame, Lord, because we have sinned against you."

DANIEL 9:7-8 (NIV)

"We paid no attention to you when you told us how to live, the clear teaching that came through your servants the prophets."

DANIEL 9:10 (THE MESSAGE)

"We kept at our sinning, never giving you a second thought, oblivious to your clear warning, and so you had no choice but to let the disaster loose on us in full force... since we persistently and defiantly ignored you."

DANIEL 9:13-14 (THE MESSAGE)

"All the neighboring nations mock Jerusalem and your people."

DANIEL 9:16 (NLT)

God's Response to Daniel

"Even while I was praying and confessing my sin and the sins of my people,desperately pleading with the Lord my God for Jerusalem, his holy mountain, Gabriel, whom I had seen in the earlier vision, flew swiftly to me at the time of the evening sacrifice and said to me, 'Daniel, I am here to help you understand God's plans. The moment you began praying a command was given. I am here to tell you what it was, for God loves you very much.'"

DANIEL 9:20-23 (TLB)

God's Promise to his People

"If my people, who are called by my name, will humble themselves and pray and seek my face and turn from their wicked ways, then I will hear from heaven, and I will forgive their sin and will heal their land."

2 CHRONICLES 7:14 (NIV)

DISCOVERY QUESTIONS:

1.) The first step of "How to Pray in a Crisis" is to let God speak to you before you speak to him. Why is that important? What difference could that make in your prayers, and even in your perspective on the "crisis"?

2.) Why do you think we sometimes hold back on our emotions when we pray to God? Why do we hesitate to state our desires and dreams to God, or to express our frustrations and anger to him?

3.) Why would the Bible warn us against saying prayers with words and phrases that we've repeated over and over again? (Hint: It's a conversation.)

4.) How have you seen your prayers and God's timing interact with each other?

PUTTING IT INTO PRACTICE:

In your prayers this week, put this verse into practice: *"You do not have what you want because you do not ask God for it"* (James 4:2 GNT).

What is your greatest desire? Talk to God about it every day this week. What is an ongoing frustration? Talk to God about it every day this week. At the end of the week, consider how you saw God move within these prayers. (God may not give you an answer by the end of the week, but where have you seen his presence?)

What are some ways you can thank God for his love and promises this week?

Mediate on God's answer to Daniel's prayer. What does it reveal to you about God?

PRAYER DIRECTION:

Do the following in your group prayer time and then on your own:

- Start by telling God you are ready to hear him, and then listen.
- Tell God that he has your undivided attention, and then listen.
- In an authentic and transparent way, express your concerns and desires to God. Let him know you are serious about your prayer, that you will continue to pray, and that you will wait for his timing on the answer.
- Thank God for the many answers to prayer he has already provided. Thank him for his love and for his promises. Ask him to help you trust him to fulfill his promises.
- Ask God to reveal to you if anything is keeping him from answering your prayers, such as sin you haven't yet confessed.
- Praise God for his grace and love, and for the way he cares about you—even the smallest details of your life.

HELP FOR HOSTS

IDEAS FOR NEW HOSTS

CONGRATULATIONS! As the host of your small group, you have responded to the call to help shepherd Jesus' flock. Few other tasks in the family of God surpass the contribution you will be making. As you prepare to facilitate your group, whether it is one session or the entire series, here are a few thoughts to keep in mind.

Remember you are not alone. God knows everything about you, and he knew you would be asked to facilitate your group. Even though you may not feel ready, this is common for all good hosts. God promises, *"I will never leave you; I will never abandon you"* (Hebrews 13:5 GNT). Whether you are facilitating for one evening, several weeks, or a lifetime, you will be blessed as you serve.

1. **DON'T TRY TO DO IT ALONE.** Pray right now for God to help you build a healthy team. If you can enlist a co-host to help you shepherd the group, you will find your experience much richer. This is your chance to involve as many people as you can in building a healthy group. All you have to do is ask people to help. You'll be surprised at the response.

2. **BE FRIENDLY AND BE YOURSELF**. God wants to use your unique gifts and temperament. Be sure to greet people at the door with a big smile . . . this can set the mood for the whole gathering. Remember, they are taking as big a step to show up at your house as you are to host a small group! Don't try to do things exactly like another host; do them in a way that fits you. Admit when you don't have an answer and apologize when you make a mistake. Your group will love you for it and you'll sleep better at night.

3. **PREPARE FOR YOUR MEETING AHEAD OF TIME.** Review the session and write down your responses to each question. Pay special attention to the **Putting It Into Practice** exercises that ask group members to do something other than engage in discussion. These exercises will help your group live out what the Bible teaches, not just talk about it.

4. **PRAY FOR YOUR GROUP MEMBERS BY NAME.** Before you begin your session, take a few moments and pray for each member by name. You may want to review the **Small Group Prayer and Praise Report** at least once a week. Ask God to use your time together to touch the heart of each person in your group. Expect God to lead

you to whomever he wants you to encourage or challenge in a special way. If you listen, God will surely lead.

5. **WHEN YOU ASK A QUESTION, BE PATIENT.** Someone will eventually respond. Sometimes people need a few moments to think about the question. After someone responds, affirm the response with a simple "thanks" or "great answer." Then ask, "How about somebody else?" or "Would someone who hasn't shared like to add anything?" Be sensitive to new people or reluctant members who aren't ready to say, pray, or do anything. If you give them a safe setting, they will blossom over time. If someone in your group is a wallflower who sits silently through every session, consider talking to them privately and encouraging them to participate. Let them know how important they are to you—that they are loved and appreciated, and that the group would value their input. Remember, still water often runs deep.
6. **PROVIDE TRANSITIONS BETWEEN QUESTIONS.** Ask if anyone would like to read the paragraph or Bible passage. Don't call on anyone, but ask for a volunteer, and then be patient until someone begins. Be sure to thank the person who reads aloud.

7. **BREAK INTO SMALLER GROUPS OCCASIONALLY.** With a greater opportunity to talk in a small circle, people will connect more with the study, apply more quickly what they're learning, and ultimately get more out of their small group experience. A small circle also encourages a quiet person to participate and tends to minimize the effects of a more vocal or dominant member.

8. **SMALL CIRCLES ARE ALSO HELPFUL DURING PRAYER TIME.** People who are unaccustomed to praying aloud will feel more comfortable trying it with just two or three others. Also, prayer requests won't take as much time, so circles will have more time to actually pray. When you gather back with the whole group, you can have one person from each circle briefly update everyone on the prayer requests from their subgroups. The other great aspect of subgrouping is that it fosters leadership development. As you ask people in the group to facilitate discussion or to lead a prayer circle, it gives them a small leadership step that can build their confidence.

9. **ROTATE FACILITATORS OCCASIONALLY.** You may be perfectly capable of hosting each time, but you will help others grow in their faith and gifts if you give them opportunities to host the group.

FREQUENTLY ASKED QUESTIONS

How long will this group meet?

This study is four sessions long. We encourage your group to add a session for a celebration. In your final session, each group member may decide if he or she desires to continue on for another study. At that time you may also want to do some informal evaluation, discuss your group guidelines, and decide which study you want to do next. We recommend you visit our website at **pastorrick.com** for more video-based small group studies.

Who is the host?

The host is the person who coordinates and facilitates your group meetings. In addition to a host, we encourage you to select one or more group members to lead your group discussions. Several other responsibilities can be rotated, including refreshments, prayer requests, worship, or keeping up with those who miss a meeting. Shared ownership in the group helps everybody grow.

Where do we find new group members?

Recruiting new members can be a challenge for groups, especially new groups with just a few people, or existing groups that lose a few people along the way. We encourage you to use the **Circles of Life** diagram on page 48 of this study guide to brainstorm a list of people from your workplace, church, school, neighborhood, family, and so on. Then pray for the people on each member's list. Allow each member to invite several people from their list. Some groups fear that newcomers will interrupt the intimacy that members have built over time. However, groups that welcome newcomers generally gain strength with the infusion of new blood. Remember, the next person you add just might become a friend for eternity. Logistically, groups find different ways to add members. Some groups remain permanently open, while others choose to open periodically, such as at the beginning or end of a study. If your group becomes too large for easy, face-to-face conversations, you can subgroup, forming a second discussion group in another room.

How do we handle the childcare needs in our group?

Childcare needs must be handled very carefully. This is a sensitive issue. We suggest you seek creative solutions as a group. One common solution is to have the adults meet in the living room and share the cost of a babysitter (or two) who can be with the kids in another part of the house.

Another popular option is to have one home for the kids and a second home (close by) for the adults. If desired, the adults could rotate the responsibility of providing a lesson for the kids. This last option is great with school-age kids and can be a huge blessing to families.

CIRCLES OF LIFE

SMALL GROUP CONNECTIONS

Discover Who You Can Connect in Community Use the chart below to help carry out one of the values in the Group Guidelines, to "Welcome Newcomers."

Follow this simple three-step process:

1. List one to two people in each circle.
2. Prayerfully select one person or couple from your list and tell your group about them.
3. Give them a call and invite them to your next meeting. Over 50 percent of those invited to a small group say, "Yes!"

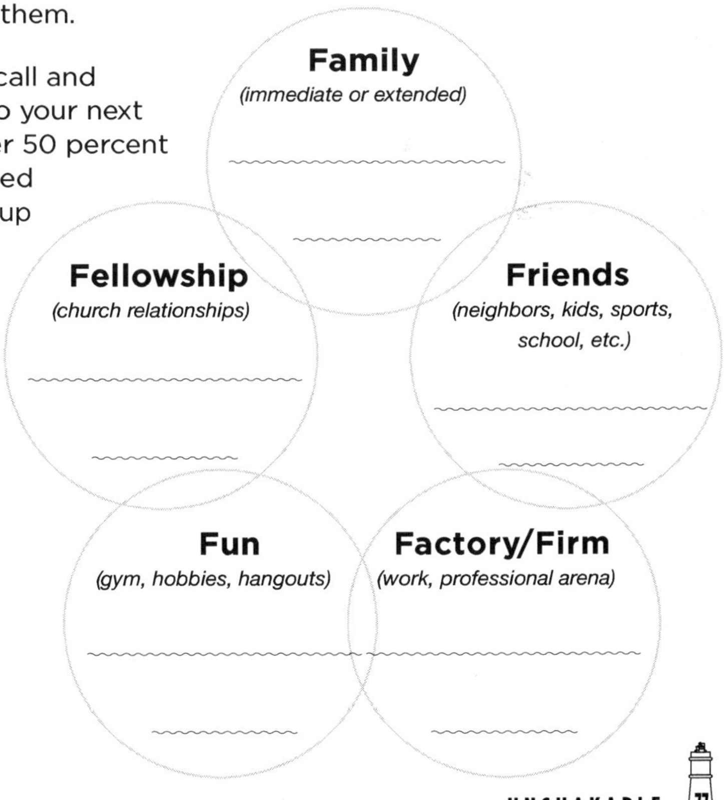

Family
(immediate or extended)

Fellowship
(church relationships)

Friends
(neighbors, kids, sports, school, etc.)

Fun
(gym, hobbies, hangouts)

Factory/Firm
(work, professional arena)

GROUP GUIDELINES

It's a good idea for every group to put words to their shared values, expectations, and commitments. Such guidelines will help you avoid unspoken agendas and unmet expectations. We recommend you discuss your guidelines during Session 1 in order to lay the foundation for a healthy group experience. Feel free to modify anything that does not work for your group.

WE AGREE TO THE FOLLOWING VALUES:

CLEAR PURPOSE	To grow healthy spiritual lives by building a healthy small group community
GROUP ATTENDANCE	To give priority to the group meeting (call if I am absent or late)
SAFE ENVIRONMENT	To create a safe place where people can be heard and feel loved (no quick answers, snap judgments, or simple fixes)
BE CONFIDENTIAL	To keep anything that is shared strictly confidential and within the group
CONFLICT RESOLUTION	To avoid gossip and to immediately resolve any concerns by following the principles of Matthew 18:15–17
SPIRITUAL HEALTH	To give group members permission to speak into my life and help me live a healthy, balanced spiritual life that is pleasing to God

LIMIT OUR FREEDOM	To limit our freedom by not serving or consuming alcohol during small group meetings or events so as to avoid causing a weaker brother or sister to stumble (1 Corinthians 8:1–13; Romans 14:19–21)
WELCOME NEWCOMERS	To invite friends who might benefit from this study and warmly welcome newcomers
BUILDING RELATIONSHIPS	To get to know the other members of the group and pray for them regularly
OTHER	______________________________ ______________________________ ______________________________

WE HAVE ALSO DISCUSSED AND AGREE ON THE FOLLOWING ITEMS:

CHILDCARE ______________________

STARTING TIME ______________________

ENDING TIME ______________________

If you haven't already done so, take a few minutes to fill out the Small Group Calendar on page 82.

SMALL GROUP PRAYER AND PRAISE REPORT

This is a place where you can write each other's requests for prayer. You can also make a note when God answers a prayer. Pray for each other's requests. If you're new to group prayer, it's okay to pray silently or to pray by using just one sentence:

"God, please help ______ to ______."

DATE/PERSON	PRAYER REQUEST	PRAISE REPORT

DATE/PERSON	PRAYER REQUEST	PRAISE REPORT

SMALL GROUP CALENDAR

Healthy groups share responsibilities and group ownership. It might take some time for this to develop. Shared ownership ensures that responsibility for the group doesn't fall to one person. Use the calendar to keep track of social events, mission projects, birthdays, or days off. Complete this calendar at your first or second meeting. Planning ahead will increase attendance and shared ownership.

DATE	LESSON	LOCATION	FACILITATOR	SNACK OR MEAL
	SESSION 1			
	SESSION 2			
	SESSION 3			
	SESSION 4			
	SESSION 5			
	SESSION 6			
	SESSION 7			
	SESSION 8			

	CELEBRATION			

ANSWER KEY

Session 1:

Before every blessing, there's a TESTING.

God tests us with STRESS before he trusts us with SUCCESS.

4 QUALITIES GOD LOOKS FOR IN YOUR LIFE

1.) INTEGRITY — Daniel never forgot who he was.
2.) DISCIPLINE — Daniel controlled his ego and his appetite.
3.) COURAGE — Daniel was willing to stand alone.
4.) HUMILITY — Daniel was tactful with authority.

HOW TO MAKE A CASE TO AN AUTHORITY

1.) Develop a reputation for RESPONSIBILITY.
2.) Be HUMBLE, not BELLIGERENT.
3.) Don't be DECEPTIVE or MANIPULATIVE.
4.) Appeal to their GOALS and INTERESTS.
5.) Choose the right PLACE, TIME, and WORDS.
6.) TRUST GOD if they reject your appeal.

Session 2:

HOW TO EXCEL IN MY EDUCATION (AND NOT LOSE MY FAITH)

1.) Decide in advance to STAND FOR GOD.
2.) Never stop LEARNING.
3.) Steep myself in GOD'S WORD.
4.) Choose BELIEVERS as my best friends.
5.) STAY CONNECTED to a church, a small group, and a ministry.
6.) Remember that God will REWARD ME.

Session 3:

WHAT TO DO WHEN YOU'RE ASKED TO DO THE IMPOSSIBLE

1.) Don't PANIC or BE AFRAID.
2.) Ask WHY.
3.) Ask for TIME to create a solution.
4.) Enlist PRAYER SUPPORT from your friends.
5.) Pray and expect God to give SUPERNATURAL HELP.
6.) WORSHIP GOD!
7.) Use what God showed you to SAVE OTHERS.
8.) POINT PEOPLE to God.

Session 4:

WHAT SHOULD I DO WHEN THE HEAT IS ON?

1.) Don't worry about DEFENDING MYSELF.

2.) Remember that God has the power to SAVE ME.

3.) BELIEVE that God will save me.

4.) I announce my LOYALTY TO GOD no matter what.

WHAT HAPPENS WHEN I TRUST GOD IN THE FURNACE?

1.) God will WALK THROUGH THE FIRE with me.

2.) God will BURN OFF everything tying me down.

3.) God will give me a new FREEDOM.

4.) God will make sure I come out UNHARMED.

5.) It will BRING UNBELIEVERS to God.

6.) God will REWARD MY FAITH in Heaven.

Session 5:

WHAT GETS US INTO TROUBLE

1.) We get COMFORTABLE and COMPLACENT with success.

2.) We don't pay attention to the WARNING SIGNS.

TO MAINTAIN SUCCESS, I NEED TO:

- REPENT
- SERVE THE POOR

3.) We put off doing WHAT WE KNOW IS RIGHT.

STEPS TO RECOVERY

1.) LOOK UP to God.

2.) Wake up to God's greatness and START WORSHIPPING.

We get better when we replace PRIDE with PRAISE.

3.) TELL OTHERS how God has saved and changed you.

Session 6:

HOW CAN I BECOME WISE LIKE DANIEL?

1.) Make a commitment to NEVER STOP LEARNING.

2.) Learn the lessons of the PRIOR GENERATIONS.

The 4 Relationships You Need to Become Wise

- MENTORS
- PARTNERS
- ROLE MODELS
- FRIENDS

3.) Maintain a HUMBLE ATTITUDE that honors God.
4.) Refuse to fill my mind with GARBAGE.
5.) Put into practice WHAT I'VE ALREADY LEARNED.
I haven't LEARNED IT until I DO IT.
If I don't HUMBLY LEARN from the generations before me,
I will end up making the EXACT SAME MISTAKES.

Session 7:

WHY WAS DANIEL UNAFRAID TO STAND OUT AND SPEAK UP FOR GOD PUBLICLY?

1.) He remembered that God was FAITHFUL in past tests.
2.) He had a CONVERSATION WITH GOD three times a day.
3.) He knew the REWARDS were greater than the RISKS.

6 WAYS I BENEFIT EVERY TIME I STAND FOR GOD

1.) It's a victory OVER FEAR.
2.) It builds my FAITH and CHARACTER.
3.) It gives God a chance to DO A MIRACLE.
4.) It encourages OTHER BELIEVERS to stand up.
5.) It's a powerful example to UNBELIEVERS.
6.) I will be REWARDED IN ETERNITY.

Session 8:

HOW TO PRAY IN A CRISIS

1.) Let God speak to me before I SPEAK TO HIM.

2 Factors to Fulfilling My Purpose in Life:

- GOD'S TIMING
- MY PRAYING

2.) Focus MY ATTENTION on God.
3.) Express my desires with EMOTION.
4.) Demonstrate my SERIOUSNESS.
5.) Thank God for his LOVE AND PROMISES.
6.) I HUMBLY CONFESS my sin.

NOTES & PRAYERS

Liz

Rita

Don

Leo 6mos

Joy 23rd

Terry Oct 24

pat Dillon nov 15?

Brenda's Mom

Olivia	Olivia
Bill Miller	Pat Dillon
Ted	Ted
Denise	Denise
nov 17 jen	jen Kyle
Connie padgent	Anita (Gary)
nancy King	Dick
Stacy Stafford	Stacy
	Connie Padgent

200700 W
Kellogg
Sat 1:00

NOTES & PRAYERS